Deep Oceans

Anna Claybourne

H www.heinemann.co.uk/library
Visit our website to find out more information about Heinemann Library b

To order:

☎ Phone 44 (0) 1865 888066

▤ Send a fax to 44 (0) 1865 314091

🖥 Visit the Heinemann Bookshop at www.heinemann.co.uk/library to browse our catalogue and order online.

Produced for Heinemann Library by
White-Thomson Publishing Ltd,
Bridgewater Business Centre,
210 High Street,
Lewes, East Sussex BN7 2NH

First published in Great Britain by Heinemann Library, Jordan Hill, Oxford OX2 8EJ, part of Harcourt Education Ltd.

Consultant: Daniel Jones
Commissioning Editors: Sarah Shannon and Steve White-Thomson
Editor: Harriet Brown
Design: Tim Mayer
Artwork: William Donohoe
Production: Duncan Gilbert

Originated by Chroma Graphics (Overseas) Pte. Ltd.
Printed in China by South China Printing Co. Ltd.

ISBN 978 0 431 90741 3
12 11 10 09 08
10 9 8 7 6 5 4 3 2 1

British Library Cataloguing in Publication Data
Claybourne, Anna
Deep oceans. – (Earth's final frontiers)
551.4'6
A full catalogue record for this book is available from the British Library.

Acknowledgements
The author and publisher would like to thank the following for allowing their pictures to be reproduced in this publication:

Corbis: **title page** (Ralph White), **11** (Jeremy Horner), **22** (Bettmann), **23** (Bettmann), **24** (Medford Historical Society Collection), **27** (Bettmann), **29** (Ralph White), **30** (Ralph White), **31** (Ralph White), **34** (Brandon D Cole), **37** (-/epa), **40–41** (Galen Rowell); Getty: **36** (AFP/Toru Yamanaka/Staff) iStock: **8** (Michael Puerzer), **16** (Cliff Parnell), **42** (Cliff Parnell), **45** (Michael Puerzer); NASA: **3, 6, 13, 39** (NASA Goddard Space Flight Center [NASA-GSFC]); Image on **33** provided courtesy of NOAA's Undersea Research Center at the University of North Carolina Wilmington; Oxford Scientific: **17** (Mark Webster), **19** (Photolibrary), **20–21** (Howard Hall), **21** (Mark Deeble and Victoria Stone), **38** (Photolibrary); Photolibrary: **40** (Animals Animals/Earth Scenes/Hamman/Heldring); Science Photo Library: **15** (B Murton/Southampton Oceanography Centre) Topfoto: **7** (Roger-Viollet), **25** (Topham Picturepoint)

Cover image of a white-eyed moray eel reproduced with permission of Science Photo Library (Matthew Oldfield, Scubazoo).

Every effort has been made to contact copyright holders of any material reproduced in this book. Any omissions will be rectified in subsequent printings if notice is given to the publishers.

CONTENTS

Words appearing in the text in bold, **like this**,
are explained in the glossary.

SEAS AND OCEANS OF THE WORLD

Arctic Ocean

ASIA

Sea of Okhotsk

Bering Sea

Sea of Japan

NORTH AMERICA

Caribbean Sea

Mariana Trench

Pacific Ocean

Coral Sea

AUSTRALIA

Tasman Sea

Pacific-Antarctic Ridge

Southern Ocean

▼ This map shows the world's main seas and oceans. Instead of just showing them as water, it shows the topography (shape) of the ocean floor. Just like land, the ocean floor has high mountains, long mountain chains, deep **trenches** and troughs, and vast plains and **basins**.

Arctic Ocean

Barents Sea

North Sea

EUROPE

ASIA

Mediterranean Sea

Atlantic Ocean

AFRICA

Arabian Sea

South China Sea

SOUTH AMERICA

Brazil Basin

Indian Ocean

Mid-Atlantic Ridge

ANTARCTICA

Weddell Sea

WHAT IS A FRONTIER?

Throughout history, humans have explored their surroundings. Over thousands of years, as transport and technology have improved, we have discovered and mapped most of our planet. We have even gone beyond the Earth, into outer space. Yet there are still some parts of Earth that remain hardly explored and little understood.

EARTH'S FINAL FRONTIERS

A "frontier" is a border or limit, beyond which lie undiscovered lands or knowledge. Earth's final frontiers are in the places that are the most difficult to travel to, and hard to survive in. They are areas of wilderness, where there are no cities, shops, or telephone cables, and the environment has never been farmed, built on, or reshaped by humans. They include the thickest, remotest jungles, the freezing polar regions, cave systems far underground – and the dark, mysterious realm of the deep oceans. Apart from space, the oceans are the greatest wilderness of all.

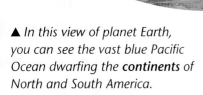

▲ *In this view of planet Earth, you can see the vast blue Pacific Ocean dwarfing the* **continents** *of North and South America.*

THE BLUE PLANET

Earth is one of the few planets that looks blue from space, thanks to the huge amounts of water covering it. Seas and oceans cover 70 percent of Earth's surface. At their deepest, the oceans are almost 11 kilometres (km) (6.8 miles) deep. In total, they contain about 1.3 billion cubic kilometres (cu km) (324 million cu miles) of water. There are more living things in the seas and oceans than in any other **habitat** on Earth.

THE WATERY DEPTHS

The seas and oceans are vast. They cover most of our planet. Besides stretching a long way around Earth, the oceans are deep. If you jumped into the water at the Mariana Trench in the Pacific Ocean, and began to sink at 3.2 kilometres per hour (kmh) (2 miles per hour [mph]), which is roughly the same speed as you walk, you would be sinking for more than 3 hours before you hit the ocean floor. The deepest oceans are more than 20 times deeper than the world's tallest building, and more than 2 km (1.2 miles) deeper than the world's tallest mountain, Mount Everest.

These depths pose huge challenges for ocean explorers. Humans need special equipment to breathe and travel underwater, and to survive the massive water pressure in the deep oceans. Technology is now beginning to solve these problems, but the oceans are so huge and deep that there are still vast areas we know very little about.

In their own words...

" ...we begin to feel the mystery and alien quality of the deep sea – the gathering darkness, the growing pressure, the starkness of a seascape in which all plant life has been left behind. "
Biologist, writer, and ecologist Rachel Carson (1907–64) describing travelling down into the depths of the ocean.

WHY EXPLORE?

Humans have a natural instinct and longing to find things out, and understand the way our world works. Many explorers seek the excitement, fame, and glory of being the first to set foot in a remote wilderness. Deep-ocean exploration can also bring valuable rewards, such as sunken treasure, or useful substances such as oil. Despite all the risks and difficulties, and the very high costs, scientists and explorers are still pushing forward the frontiers of deep-ocean discovery.

◀ A painting of Marco Polo (1254–1324), a famous 13th-century explorer, going ashore after a journey by ship. He travelled across Europe and Asia by both land and sea.

WATERY WORLD

The seas and oceans are a hugely important part of Earth's history and geology. They formed more than four billion years ago, when the Earth was very young. The shape of the oceans and the ocean floor has changed a great deal over that time.

WHERE DID THE OCEANS COME FROM?

The Earth is thought to have formed about 4.5 billion years ago from a swirling mass of gases, ice, and dust orbiting around the sun. As it formed a solid ball, water vapour (water in the form of a gas) was forced out from inside the planet, and collected on the surface as liquid water. More water arrived when comets, which are largely made of ice, crashed into the young planet.

▼ A comet is a ball of ice and dust that gives off gases as it zooms through space. In the past, comets have collided with the Earth and deposited water on the Earth's surface.

WHY IS SEAWATER SALTY?

As rivers flow to the oceans, they carry small amounts of salt and other minerals with them, dissolved from the rocks over which they flow. This salt collects in the seas and oceans and, when water **evaporates**, the salt is left behind. There are also vents and **seeps** on the ocean floor. At these openings, hot water from inside Earth flows into the oceans, carrying dissolved salts with it. Besides being about 3.5 percent salt, seawater also contains small amounts of many other minerals, including gold.

CRUST AND OCEAN FLOOR

The Earth's surface is made up of a hard, rocky crust floating on a layer of fluid rock, called magma. There are two kinds of crust – **continental crust** and **oceanic crust**. Oceanic crust is made of denser, heavier rocks, so it sinks lower into the magma. The Earth's water flows down into these lower areas, forming the seas and oceans.

THE SEAS AND OCEANS

What is the difference between a sea and an ocean? In fact, all seas and oceans are part of the same huge body of water, encircling the globe. Very large, open parts are usually called oceans, while seas are smaller areas, partly enclosed by land. There are five oceans – the Pacific Ocean (the biggest of all), the Atlantic Ocean, the Indian Ocean, the Southern Ocean, and the Arctic Ocean. There are more than 120 smaller seas and other sea-like areas of water called **gulfs**, bays, and **straits**. Each of these are part of one of the oceans. For example, the South China Sea lies between China, the Philippines, Vietnam, and Borneo, and is part of the Pacific Ocean.

TECTONIC PLATES

Earth's crust is made up of huge sections called **tectonic plates**, which fit together like jigsaw pieces. They gradually move and jostle around, causing the continents and oceans to change shape over time. Like the land, the ocean floor has many geographical features, especially at places where two plates meet. Long, high oceanic **ridges** form where two plates are being pushed apart by new magma from inside Earth. In other places, one plate pushes beneath another, forming a deep trench. There are also underwater mountains, volcanoes, valleys, and plains.

▼ *This cross-section picture shows how continental and oceanic crust make up the Earth's land and ocean floor.*

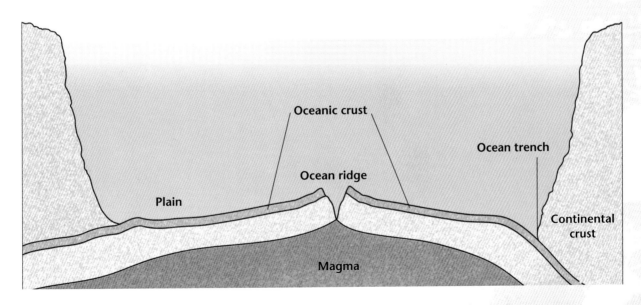

Oceanic crust

Ocean trench

Ocean ridge

Plain

Continental crust

Magma

THE CHANGING OCEANS

The water in the seas and oceans is constantly moving, flowing, and swirling around. Waves, **currents**, and tides have a huge effect on planet Earth. They influence the weather, wildlife, fishing, and shipping, and can even cause deadly disasters.

CURRENTS

A current is a stream of flowing water within a sea or ocean. There are networks of huge currents flowing around the world's seas and oceans. They carry warm water into cooler areas, and vice versa. The water in a typical current moves about 10 km (6 miles) each day.

Currents affect the climate by changing the temperature of the oceans. For example, the Gulf Stream current flows northward from the warm tropical part of the Atlantic Ocean to the seas around the British Isles and Iceland, making these countries much warmer than they would be otherwise. Currents also make it easier for ships and marine animals to travel across the oceans.

OCEAN CIRCULATION

Scientists think that currents on the surface of the oceans are caused by winds. They tend to move from the warm waters around the equator towards the North and South Poles. As the water reaches the Poles, it cools and becomes denser and heavier. It sinks down to the ocean floor, creating deep-ocean currents that flow back towards the equator. In this way, currents of water circulate around and around in the oceans.

▼ *This map shows the world's main surface ocean currents. Cold-water currents are shown in blue, and warm-water currents are shown in red.*

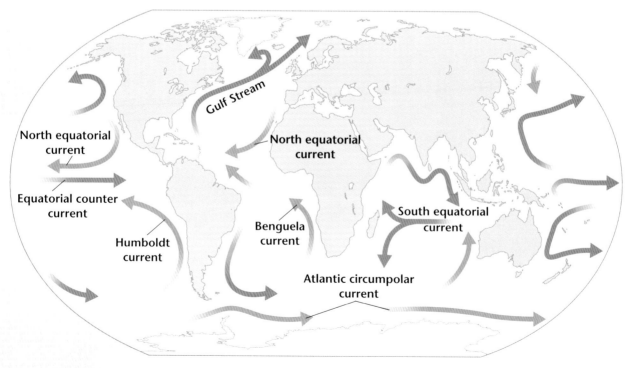

North equatorial current

Equatorial counter current

Humboldt current

Gulf Stream

North equatorial current

Benguela current

South equatorial current

Atlantic circumpolar current

WAVES

Ocean waves are made by the wind pushing at water on the surface of the sea. Waves are a form of energy. They travel forwards through the water, making it rise up as they pass by, but they do not move the water itself forwards. When a wave reaches shallow water, it drags on the ocean bed and tips forwards. This is why waves break on the beach. There are waves on the oceans all the time, but sometimes storms or **tsunamis** cause extra-large waves that can flatten coastal towns and villages, and flood the land.

TSUNAMIS FROM THE OCEAN FLOOR

A tsunami happens when a large amount of seawater moves suddenly. Most tsunamis are caused by earthquakes on the deep ocean floor. This sets up a series of fast waves shooting off in all directions, like ripples in a pond. When a tsunami wave reaches the shore, it slows down and piles up into a very high, extremely dangerous wave that crashes on to the land.

▲ *A tsunami wave crashes on to the coast of Thailand. It was part of a huge tsunami that devastated coasts around the Indian Ocean on 26 December 2004.*

FOOD FROM THE DEEP

The water in the deep oceans contains lots of nutrients (food chemicals). They come from dead **plankton** and other marine organisms that have sunk down through the depths. In parts of the ocean, especially near the Poles, powerful winds and waves mix the water, bringing the nutrients up from the depths to the surface. This is called upwelling, and it provides plenty of food for whales, fish, and other marine animals.

OCEANS, WEATHER, AND CLIMATE

The seas and oceans are closely connected to the Earth's weather. Rain and other **precipitation** comes from water that has evaporated from the oceans. In turn, the climate affects the oceans – warmer temperatures make sea levels rise, and increase the number of ocean storms.

THE WATER CYCLE

Rivers are constantly flowing into the oceans, so where does all the water go? The world's water is constantly moving around in a huge water cycle. The warmth of the sun makes some of the oceans' water evaporate into a gas – water vapour. It rises into the air, cools, and **condenses** into droplets that form clouds. The clouds blow over the land, and the water in them falls as rain. The rain flows into rivers, and eventually back into the oceans. Every year, more than 400,000 cu km (100,000 cu miles) of seawater evaporates into the air.

OCEAN STORMS

Hurricanes (also called **typhoons** or **cyclones** in some parts of the world) are the most powerful and dangerous of all storms. They start out over the oceans when the sun heats up the water, making a mass of warm, damp air rise up above the surface. This sucks in more air from the surrounding area, and as it rushes inwards, it begins to swirl around in a spiral. The giant spiral of gale-force winds and rain clouds moves across the ocean, sometimes blowing onto the land before dying away.

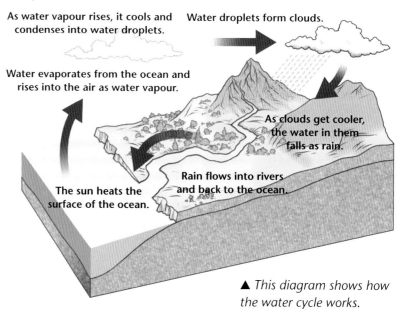

Wind blows the clouds over the land.

As water vapour rises, it cools and condenses into water droplets.

Water droplets form clouds.

Water evaporates from the ocean and rises into the air as water vapour.

As clouds get cooler, the water in them falls as rain.

Rain flows into rivers and back to the ocean.

The sun heats the surface of the ocean.

▲ *This diagram shows how the water cycle works.*

OCEAN SCIENCE

There are many different kinds of science that can be involved in the study of the oceans. Here are a few of them:

Oceanography – The study of the seas and oceans

Marine biology – The study of sea animals and plants

Sedimentology – The study of how **sediment**, such as mud and sand, settles and collects in layers, especially on the seabed

Marine ecology – The study of ocean habitats and communities of living things

Marine paleontology – The study of sea fossils.

CHANGING SEA LEVELS

Earth's climate affects the temperature of the seas and oceans, and this alters the sea level – the height of the surface of the oceans and seas around the world. Sea levels have changed many times throughout Earth's history. Around 20,000 years ago, for example, the world was in an **ice age**. Much more of its water was locked up in ice around the Arctic and Antarctic, and the sea level was lower than today. At the moment, the Earth is heating up. This is mainly because of global warming caused by gases released into the air when we burn fuel.

When Earth gets warmer, the sea level rises for two main reasons. Firstly, **ice caps** and **glaciers** melt, adding water to the oceans. Secondly, as water gets warmer, it expands, and takes up more space. Over the past 18,000 years or so, the sea level has risen by about 120 metres (m) (400 feet [ft]). As the sea level rises, the oceans cover more of the land, changing the shape of the coast.

SUNKEN LANDS

In some places, there are underwater buildings and settlements that have been covered by the rising oceans. For example, old stone walls dating from the Bronze Age, more than 2,500 years ago, can be seen under the sea near the Scilly Isles, off southwestern Britain. Since they were built, the sea level has risen over them. At Mahabalipuram in India, there are ancient temples on the seabed a short distance from the shore.

▼ *This **satellite** image shows a tropical storm growing into a hurricane, named Hurricane Claudette, off the coast of Texas, USA. You can see the coastline at the bottom left of the picture.*

THE OCEAN FRONTIER

Humans have used boats to explore the surface of the oceans for thousands of years, and diving equipment has allowed us to explore shallower waters. The true final ocean frontier is the deep ocean. It holds many mysteries that scientists and explorers are still trying to uncover. But why are some parts of the oceans so much deeper than others – and how deep counts as the deep ocean?

THE SHAPE OF THE OCEANS

Most seas and oceans have a similar shape in cross-section. Next to the land, the ocean floor is smooth and slopes gently downwards. This is the **continental shelf**, and it can range from just a few kilometres to hundreds of kilometres wide. The water here is usually less than 150 m (500 ft) deep.

At the **continental slope**, the ocean floor angles much more steeply downwards. Then, the slope becomes more gentle again, forming the **continental rise**. This leads down to the **abyssal plain**, the deep, flat ocean floor, which is around 2,000–5,000 m (7,000–17,000 ft) deep.

▼ *The top 200 m (650 ft) is called the **sunlit zone** because sunlight can penetrate the water. The **twilight zone** is between 200 m and 1,000 m (640–3,300 ft) deep and receives very little sunlight. The next three zones – the **dark zone**, the **abyssal zone**, and the **hadal zone** – receive no sunlight at all.*

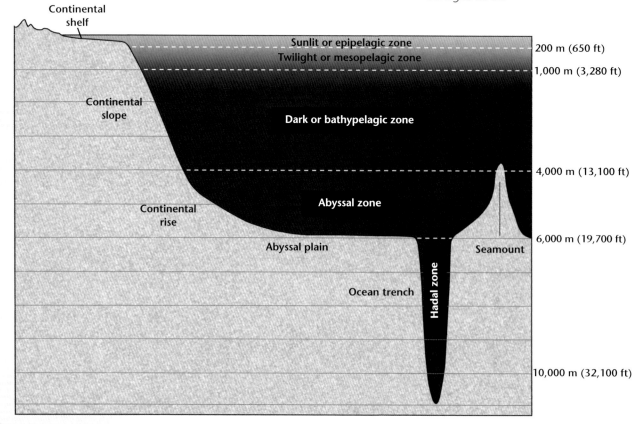

The deepest parts of the oceans are found in ocean trenches, where two tectonic plates meet (see page 9). Where there are high ridges on the ocean floor, the ocean is shallower. The depth of the ocean can also change suddenly where an underwater mountain (**seamount**) rises from the ocean floor, sometimes reaching all the way to the ocean surface and forming an island.

▲ *This view is of the ocean floor 3,500 m (11,480 ft) below the surface. The only light is coming from the* **submersible** *that has taken the photo.*

HOW DEEP IS DEEP?

The deep ocean is usually defined as the ocean below a depth of 200 m (650 ft). This is the point at which little or no sunlight can penetrate. As the average depth of the oceans is around 3,800 m (12,500 ft), the vast majority of the ocean counts as "deep". However, only a few small areas plunge into the **hadal zone**, below a depth of 6,000 m (20,000 ft). This zone accounts for just two percent of the ocean floor. In the deepest oceans, it is totally dark and the pressure of the water above is huge.

In their own words...

"The bottom appeared light and clear, a waste of snuff-coloured ooze. Indifferent to the nearly 200,000 tons of pressure clamped on her metal sphere, the *Trieste* balanced herself delicately on the few pounds of guide rope that lay on the bottom, making token claim... to the ultimate depths in all our oceans – the Challenger Deep... And as we were settling this final fathom, I saw a wonderful thing. Lying on the bottom just beneath us was some type of flatfish, resembling a sole, about one foot long and six inches across. Even as I saw him, his two round eyes on top of his head spied us – a monster of steel – invading his silent realm."

Jacques Piccard (born 1922), who along with Don Walsh (born 1931), became the first to visit the bottom of Challenger Deep, the deepest point in the oceans.

WHAT LIES BENEATH?

If the deep oceans are one of Earth's final frontiers, still waiting to be properly explored, then what might we find there? The oceans could contain many different surprises, resources, and scientific knowledge.

WILDLIFE

In the vast expanses of the deep oceans, animals can hide from humans far more easily than on land. Deep-ocean fishing crews and explorers regularly find previously unrecorded species – even large ones such as sharks. Some experts estimate that there are millions of species in the oceans still unknown to science.

UNDERSTANDING THE OCEAN FLOOR

Some scientists explore the deep to study the features of the ocean floor, such as trenches, ridges, and **hydrothermal vents**, where hot water seeps out from inside Earth (see pages 30–31).

These geological features can provide clues about how Earth formed, and how tectonic plates work. As well as increasing our knowledge, this can help with practical problems such as predicting earthquakes.

SCIENCE CLUES

Studying the ocean floor can help scientists find out about other areas of science, too. For example, the way layers of sediment have settled on the ocean floor can show where **asteroids** landed on Earth millions of years ago.

HOW FOSSILS FORM

Fossils form most easily in the seas and oceans because of the layers of sediment (mud, sand, and **silt**) that quickly collect on the ocean floor, covering up the remains of dead animals. Because of this, the most common fossils are of marine animals, such as fish and ammonites. This step-by-step sequence describes how a fossil forms.

1. A dead animal falls to the ocean floor.
2. Its soft parts rot away, leaving the skeleton or shell.
3. Layers of sediment settle on top. Over time, they are squashed down and harden into rock.
4. The hard parts of the animal gradually dissolve, leaving a hollow mould.
5. Mineral-rich seawater fills up the space, and minerals in the water collect there, making a stone cast – a fossil.

▼ *These are fossils of ammonites. Ammonites were a type of prehistoric sea animal related to octopuses and squid, but with a spiral shell. They lived between 400 million and 65 million years ago.*

Fossils found on or under the ocean floor tell us about prehistoric life. Measuring deep-ocean temperatures and currents lets scientists track how fast the climate is changing.

▲ *A diver explores the sunken wreck of an old yacht in the Red Sea.*

Patterns of magnetic fields in the ocean floor have even revealed that Earth's magnetic field has reversed many times, and may soon do so again. Compass needles will point to the South Pole in Antarctica, instead of to the North Pole in the Arctic.

HIDDEN TREASURE

Some parts of the deep oceans could be sources of precious stones or other useful minerals, and there are valuable deposits of oil under the ocean floor. Commercial explorers (**prospectors**) are always looking for these as a way to make money. The deep ocean floor is also home to thousands of sunken ships, such as the RMS *Titanic* (see pages 30–31). Many could reveal historical secrets, and some still contain precious cargoes of gold and gemstones, antique pottery, or carvings.

SECRETS OF THE SHALLOW SEAS

Although the deepest oceans hold the most secrets, scientists are still making discoveries in the shallow seas as well. In 2006, they explored a little-known coral reef near the coast of Papua in Indonesia, and discovered dozens of previously unknown fish and coral species.

CHALLENGES OF DEEP-OCEAN EXPLORATION

There are many reasons why the oceans – especially the deep oceans – are so difficult and dangerous to explore. These challenges have forced humans to stay close to the surface for centuries. Only within the last 100 years have we begun to overcome them, and discover the deep ocean.

OXYGEN

Humans, like all animals, need to breathe oxygen. We have lungs that extract oxygen from the air. Although water contains oxygen too, our lungs cannot extract it. Marine animals have organs called gills to filter oxygen from the water. To spend more than a few minutes underwater, we have to take an air or oxygen supply with us. Deep-ocean exploration vehicles (submersibles) carry a supply of compressed oxygen in heavy tanks. However, this limits the amount of time that they can spend underwater. If anything goes wrong and the explorers get stuck, the oxygen will start to run out, leaving them in big trouble.

FREEZING AND BOILING

In the coldest, deepest parts of the ocean, the water can be freezing cold – or even just below freezing. (It stays liquid because water expands when it freezes, and the water pressure in the deep ocean stops it from expanding.) Yet around hydrothermal vents (see pages 30–31), the water can be boiling hot. These temperatures are dangerous to humans, so submersibles have to protect their passengers. Changing temperatures can also damage machines by making their metal parts expand and contract (shrink), so they have to be built to cope with this without breaking. They must also be made of materials that are resistant to salty seawater, as it can eat away at metals and damage them.

▼ When a submersible is in the deepest parts of the sea, there are thousands of metres of seawater pressing down on top of it.

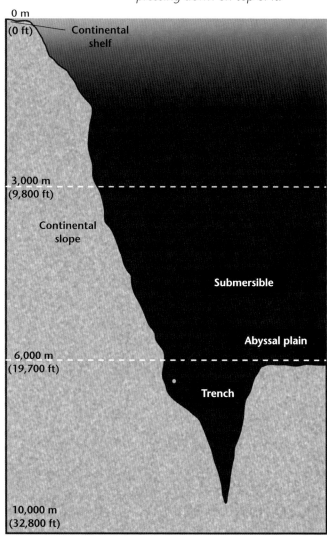

0 m
(0 ft) — Continental shelf

3,000 m
(9,800 ft)

Continental slope

Submersible

Abyssal plain

6,000 m
(19,700 ft)

Trench

10,000 m
(32,800 ft)

STAYING IN TOUCH

Underwater explorers need to stay in contact with the surface in case of an emergency. Early diving vessels used telephone wires leading up to a ship on the surface. Today, submersibles use radio to communicate, which allows them to move more freely without being tied to one place.

WHERE ARE YOU?

In the darkness of the deep ocean, without any roads, or even the sun or stars to follow, underwater vessels need a way to get back to the shore, or to their support ship. They cannot use GPS (global positioning system) technology while underwater because seawater blocks the signals that GPS units send to satellites. One of the best systems uses devices called **transponders**, which keep the ship and the submersible informed of each other's whereabouts.

CABIN FEVER

Being thousands of metres underwater in a tiny chamber can be horribly **claustrophobic**. Deep-ocean explorers have to be calm, mentally strong, and very brave. Could you handle it?

▲ *The Johnson Sea Link submersible being launched from its base ship. There are oxygen tanks, lights, and communication equipment attached to it.*

In their own words...

"First of all there was the complete and utter loneliness and isolation, a feeling wholly unlike the isolation felt when removed from fellow men by mere distance... It was a loneliness more akin to a first venture upon the Moon or Venus. "

Pioneer undersea explorer, William Beebe (1877–1962), compares exploring the deep ocean in his tiny diving vessel, the **bathysphere** (see pages 26–27), to travelling in outer space.

HOW TRANSPONDERS WORK

A transponder is a device that can send out and detect sounds. Before a deep-ocean exploration mission, three or more transponders are dropped to the ocean floor in the area of the dive. As the submersible moves around under water, it sends out a repeated sound or "ping". Each transponder detects it and sends another sound back. Computers on board use the time taken for the sounds to return to calculate the position of the vessel in relation to the transponders.

UNDER PRESSURE

Even if you can solve the problems of exploring in cold, dark, salty water, using special gear to help you breathe, find your way, and stay in touch with the surface, there's still one more problem to contend with – water pressure. The water pressure in the deepest oceans is so great that it would crush and kill an unprotected human in a second.

HOW WATER PRESSURE WORKS

The water in the world's oceans is held down by gravity, which pulls everything towards the middle of the Earth. The deeper you go under water, the more water there is above you. The weight of all the water pushes downwards, and squeezes you from all sides. Humans are built to breathe air at sea level, where the air pressure measures one **atmosphere atm** (a unit of pressure). For every 10 m (33 ft) you go down, the water pressure increases by one atmosphere. At 10 m (33 ft) below the surface, the water pressure is two atmospheres, or twice surface pressure. At 100 m (330 ft) deep, it is 11 atmospheres. At the very bottom of the sea, 10,910 m (35,800 ft) down, the pressure is 1,092 atmospheres.

BREATHING PROBLEMS

Deep-ocean animals have special **adaptations** that allow them to cope with water pressure. Deep-diving whales, for example, can collapse their lungs safely. However, humans cannot do this. Without special equipment, it is impossible to breathe in water more than a few metres deep, even with an air supply. The water pressure squeezes your chest so hard that you can't suck any air in. At depths of 100 m (330 ft), the pressure squashes your lungs to the size of your fists, and can damage your heart. Some divers do dive deeper than this, but they need hi-tech gear, and it is still very dangerous.

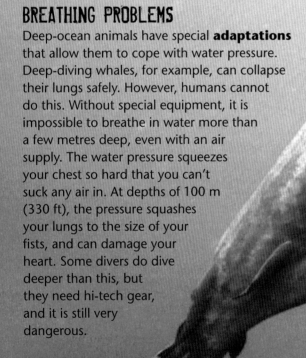

WHO'S WHO

Blaise Pascal

French scientist Blaise Pascal (1623–62) was one of the first to study and understand pressure in fluids (such as air and water). He noticed that air pressure was lower at high altitudes, and discovered how water and air push in at an object from all sides. Pascal's Law states that at any particular depth in a fluid, the pressure will always be the same. At 10 m (33 ft) underwater anywhere in the world, the pressure will always be the same.

▼ *Sperm whales are mammals and breathe air, but they can hold their breath and dive to depths greater than 2,000 m (6,500 ft) to hunt. Their bodies are not damaged by the water pressure.*

SUBMERSIBLES

Because of the immense water pressure, humans can only visit the deepest oceans inside very strong deep-ocean submersibles. A normal submarine would be squashed flat. Submersibles have a spherical passenger chamber made of iron or steel. This is the strongest shape for resisting pressure from all directions. Any windows must be made from very thick glass, plastic, or quartz crystal. The submersible must be 100 percent leak-proof and crack-proof. If it broke, the water pressure would crush anyone inside instantly.

ANOTHER WAY

All these challenges mean that building deep-ocean exploration vessels that can carry passengers safely is incredibly difficult and expensive. Therefore, explorers often do things another way – remotely. They can explore the ocean floor from ships on the surface, using sonar (see page 25), or equipment lowered down on cables. They also use ROVs (remotely operated vehicles). These are robot submersibles with no crew, controlled from the surface by radio signals. An ROV can film its surroundings and use robotic arms to collect ocean floor samples. We can also now find out a lot about things such as ocean temperature and depth from information recorded by satellites orbiting Earth.

▲ *In this submersible, the spherical passenger chamber is made of clear acrylic, giving the crew an all-round view.*

HISTORY OF DEEP-OCEAN EXPLORATION

The first ocean explorations took place on the surface of the oceans. People have been using ocean-going boats for at least 40,000 years for exploration, travel, and fishing. But no one knew how deep the oceans were, or even how far they reached. Until as recently as the 15th century, many people thought that Earth was flat, and that if they sailed too far, they might fall off the edge!

THE FIRST DIVERS

The earliest divers simply held their breath and plunged into the water to catch fish or look for pearls. To this day, there are still pearl divers who dive without any breathing equipment to collect pearls from oyster shells. Gradually, though, people began to invent devices to help them dive. Hollowed-out animal horns made early snorkels or breathing tubes, allowing divers to breathe air from the surface with their heads submerged.

The ancient Greeks used simple **diving bells** – large pots that could carry a pocket of air underwater with the diver. The Greek leader, Alexander the Great (356–323 BCE), even had a glass diving barrel made, which he used to view underwater life. In 1620, Dutch inventor, Cornelius Drebbel (1572–1633), built the first submarine, which was wooden and powered by oars.

HOW A DIVING BELL WORKS

A diving bell is a strong, heavy, hollow diving vessel shaped like a bell. When it is lowered into the water, it traps air inside it, allowing humans to breathe under water. In ancient times, divers used diving bells as an underwater base, holding their breath to go out to catch fish, then coming back to the bell to get their breath back.

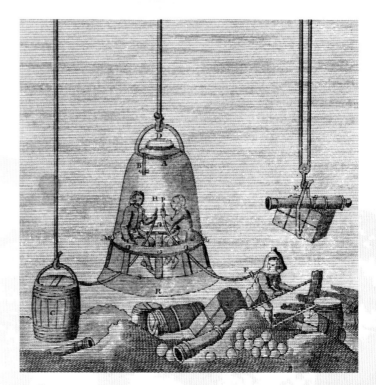

▲ Trapped air inside the bell holds the water down, stopping it from flowing up into the bell.

In their own words...

" One can allow divers to breathe by lowering a bronze tank into the water. It will not fill up with water, but keeps its air when lowered vertically. **"**

Ancient Greek scientist and writer, Aristotle (384–322 BCE), describes diving bells being used in the 4th century BCE.

WHO'S WHO

Jacques Cousteau

Jacques Cousteau (1910–97) was a famous French diver, underwater explorer, and film-maker. As well as working on the aqualung, he explored the world's oceans, diving from his ship the *Calypso*, and developed new underwater filming techniques.

DIVING SUITS

The first proper diving suit was invented by a German, Augustus Siebe (1788–1872), in 1837. He pumped air from the surface into the helmet of the suit, which allowed the diver to breathe easily. Divers could now breathe at deeper depths, but they were still tied to the surface by the air supply cable. Later, divers began taking canisters of pure oxygen with them, but too much oxygen can be dangerous. In 1943, French divers Jacques Cousteau (1910–97) and Emile Gagnan (1900–79) developed the **aqualung**. This has a self-contained air supply with a valve to allow the air through at the right pressure for breathing. Now, divers were free to explore safely under water.

A NEW WORLD

These inventions revealed all kinds of secrets of the seas – amazing wildlife, coral reefs, sunken wrecks, and underwater cliffs, caves, and other stunning features of the ocean floor. But diving suits and bells couldn't resist water pressure well enough to explore the deepest depths of the oceans.

▼ *Famous underwater explorer Jacques Cousteau (centre) is shown here preparing for a dive. He's using wetsuits and aqualung (also known as **scuba**) gear, which he helped to invent.*

OCEAN FLOOR DISCOVERIES

Humans did not actually visit the depths of the oceans until well into the 20th century. Before that, they invented other ways of finding out what was at the bottom of the seas and oceans and how deep they were.

SOUNDING

Sounding means measuring the depth of water. This was first done using a long cable with a lead weight. This was lowered off a ship until it touched the ocean floor. The length of cable that had been lowered showed the depth of the ocean. By taking soundings in lots of different places, scientists could build up a picture of the shape of the ocean floor over a large area.

This method wasn't ideal because a strong current could drag the cable sideways, making the measurement greater than it should be. However, United States navy officer Matthew Fontaine Maury (1806–73) still made history when he used cable sounding to make the first ever ocean-floor map, which showed the floor of the North Atlantic Ocean, in 1855. This was the start of the science of **bathymetry**, which means measuring and charting the shape and features of the ocean floor.

▶ *This photograph shows Matthew Fontaine Maury. He was internationally acclaimed for his contributions to ocean science and ocean navigation.*

▲ *Charles Wyville Thomson (seated second from right, all in white) with other members of the crew on board HMS* Challenger.

WHAT'S GOING ON DOWN THERE?

Also in the 19th century, scientists began to study other aspects of the oceans from the surface. German-Estonian scientist Emil von Lenz (1804–65) studied the content of seawater, and measured the temperature of deep ocean water to find out how currents work. Charles Wyville Thomson (1830–82) used deep-ocean dredging equipment to collect wildlife from depths of 1,200 m (4,000 ft), proving that animals could live there.

THE CHALLENGER EXPEDITION

This work kick-started a new fascination with what lay under the oceans, and the science of oceanography – the study of the seas and oceans – began to take off. Wyville Thomson persuaded the British navy to provide a ship for scientists to use for their explorations. The ship, HMS *Challenger*, sailed the world from 1872 to 1876. The crew and scientists on board mapped the ocean floor, collected samples of rocks and deep-ocean wildlife, and made records of the patterns of ocean currents.

WHO'S WHO

Charles Wyville Thomson

Charles Wyville Thomson was a Scottish naturalist. After working as a professor of natural history and geology, he began to study deep-ocean wildlife. He arranged the first *Challenger* expedition, and was the chief scientist on board. After returning, Thomson was made a knight and spent the rest of his life writing about his adventures and the discoveries he made.

SOUNDING BY SONAR

In the early 20th century, scientists developed sonar. This is a way of measuring distances by sending out pings (pulses of sound) then measuring how long an echo takes to bounce back. Sonar makes it possible to measure the depth and shape of the ocean floor very accurately, because it is not affected by currents. Between 1932 and 1954, another survey ship, HMS *Challenger II*, used sonar to make a new map of the ocean floor. It also identified the deepest point in the oceans, Challenger Deep, which was named after HMS *Challenger II*.

EXPLORING THE DEPTHS

As the 20th century dawned, no human had ever visited the deep ocean and returned alive. The dangers of water pressure meant that even the deepest dives, using armoured diving suits, had only reached about 160 m (525 ft). The deepest oceans are at least 60 times deeper than that. But explorers were determined to go there.

In their own words...

" As fish after fish swam into my restricted line of vision – fish which heretofore I had seen only dead and in my nets – as I saw their colours ... their activities and modes of swimming ... I felt that all the trouble and cost and risk were repaid. "
William Beebe describing his first dive in the bathysphere.

DREAMING OF THE DEEP

William Beebe was a famous American wildlife expert in the 1920s. He often went exploring and diving to look at animals, and wrote a series of books about his discoveries. He was fascinated by the strange animals that fishing boats hauled up from the deep ocean, and he longed to see them in the wild. Then, in 1928, a friend introduced Beebe to Otis Barton (1899–1992), an engineer who had come up with a design for a deep-ocean diving machine.

THE BRILLIANT BATHYSPHERE

Beebe loved Barton's design. It was a steel sphere, the strongest shape for resisting water pressure. It would be lowered hundreds of metres into the ocean from a boat, with a crew of two inside. Beebe named it a "bathysphere", meaning "deep sphere", and the two men worked together to get it built. To make it light enough, the bathysphere had to be small – the final model measured just 144 cm (57 in) across. After testing it with no crew, Beebe and Barton squeezed inside and made their first dive on 6 May 1931.

They descended to 244 m (800 ft) – deeper than any human being had been before. And on 15 August 1834, they made their deepest dive of all, to 923 m (3,028 ft). Beebe was thrilled to see weird deep-ocean fish and shrimps through the sphere's porthole.

INSIDE THE BATHYSPHERE

The bathysphere was equipped with an oxygen supply and a telephone link to the surface. This diagram shows what it was like inside.

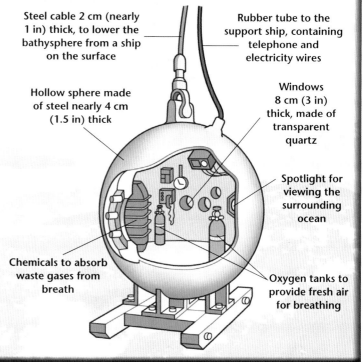

Steel cable 2 cm (nearly 1 in) thick, to lower the bathysphere from a ship on the surface

Rubber tube to the support ship, containing telephone and electricity wires

Hollow sphere made of steel nearly 4 cm (1.5 in) thick

Windows 8 cm (3 in) thick, made of transparent quartz

Spotlight for viewing the surrounding ocean

Chemicals to absorb waste gases from breath

Oxygen tanks to provide fresh air for breathing

GOING DEEPER

Beebe and Barton had revolutionized ocean exploration – but there was still a long way to go. Since the bathysphere was tethered to a ship, it could not explore freely. And there were still much deeper parts of the ocean to visit. In the 1930s, Swiss inventor Auguste Piccard (1884–1962) set out to build an even better diving machine. His invention was called a **bathyscaphe**, or "deep boat". It had a sphere for the crew to sit in, like the bathysphere. But instead of hanging on a cable, the sphere was attached to a tank full of petrol, which is lighter than water. Piccard could make the bathyscaphe sink or rise in the ocean by attaching or removing iron weights.

In 1960, Piccard's second bathyscaphe, the *Trieste*, made the deepest dive ever. It carried Piccard's son, Jacques, and a United States navy officer, Don Walsh, 10,911 m (35,797 ft) to the bottom of Challenger Deep in the Pacific Ocean. They saw small fish swimming away from them, and noticed that the ocean floor was covered in a slimy substance, which oceanographers call ooze. It is made up of the remains of dead plankton that has drifted down to the ocean floor.

WHO'S WHO

Auguste Piccard

Auguste Piccard (1884–1962) was born in Basel, Switzerland, and became a professor of physics at the University of Brussels, in Belgium. Besides being a scientist, he was a famous balloonist. In 1932, Auguste flew a balloon to a record-breaking 16,916 m (55,500 ft). He used his knowledge of balloons to design the bathyscaphe, making it work in a similar way.

▼ *Auguste Piccard stands on the* Trieste, *the bathyscaphe he built, which was to make the deepest ever ocean dive.*

MODERN DEEP-OCEAN EXPLORATION

In the 1960s, scientists developed a new generation of deep-ocean craft, the submersibles. Designed to be smaller and easier to steer than the bathyscaphe, they are still used for exploring the deep oceans today.

ALVIN LEADS THE WAY

The first of the submersibles, *Alvin*, was completed in 1964 and is still being used today. It is named after Allyn Vine, a scientist at Woods Hole Oceanographic Institute in Massachusetts, USA, who first promoted the idea of a new kind of deep-ocean vessel. *Alvin* has a hull about 7 m (23 ft) long, built around a pressure-resistant spherical passenger chamber about 2 m (6.5 ft) in diameter. It can carry three people. From inside the spherical chamber, the crew can control *Alvin's* lights, cameras, and its two robotic arms for collecting samples or doing experiments.

In their own words...

"The animals are amazing and I feel just as excited now as the first time I saw them more than 15 years ago. Each time we go down is new, and we never know what we will find and how it will affect the research we are doing."

Oceanographer Dr. Craig Cary (born 1954) describes seeing deep-ocean wildlife from on board the submersible *Alvin*.

INSIDE ALVIN

This cutaway diagram shows the main working parts of the *Alvin* submersible, including the passenger hull or sphere.

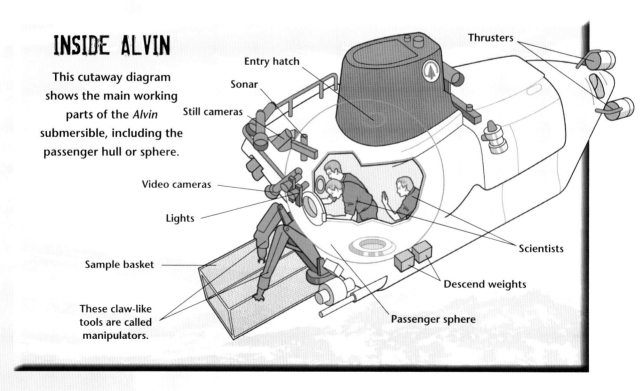

Thrusters

Entry hatch

Sonar

Still cameras

Video cameras

Lights

Sample basket

These claw-like tools are called manipulators.

Scientists

Descend weights

Passenger sphere

A mission in *Alvin* usually takes about eight hours – two hours to descend into the deep ocean, four hours exploring, filming, sampling, or experimenting, and another two hours returning to the surface.

MORE SUBMERSIBLES AND ROVS

Here are a few of the exploration vessels currently exploring the deep oceans:

ACCIDENTAL DISCOVERY

In 1968, *Alvin* sank after its tether broke. The three crew on board managed to escape to safety by scrambling out of the passenger chamber, though one broke his ankle. *Alvin* was lost on the ocean floor, 1,525 m (5,000 ft) down, for 3 months. When it was recovered, scientists found that a sandwich left on board had not rotted away. This revealed that organic material can be preserved for longer in the deep ocean than at sea level. Scientists think this is because of the freezing cold temperatures and the low levels of oxygen in very deep water.

Johnson Sea Link submersible

There are two Johnson Sea Link submersibles, *JSL I* and *JSL II*. Each one can dive to about 900 m (almost 3,000 ft) and has two small passenger chambers. One chamber is made entirely from clear acrylic, giving a panoramic view for observing and filming wildlife. *JSL I* and *JSL II* cannot dive as deep as some submersibles, but they are at the forefront of deep-ocean exploration.

Nautile submersible

The *Nautile*, a French submersible, is specially designed for very deep ocean exploration. It can carry a crew of three down to a depth of around 6,000 m (19,700 ft).

Shinkai 6500 submersible

Shinkai 6500 is a Japanese submersible that holds the record for the deepest dive by any submersible in current use. In 1989, it reached a depth of 6,527 m (21,415 ft) in the Japan Trench, in the Pacific Ocean.

▲ Alvin *exploring the ocean floor, seen through the porthole of another submersible.* Alvin's *maximum diving depth is 4,500 m (14,674 ft).*

Jason ROV

Jason is an ROV (remotely operated vehicle). It is a crewless robot craft that operates while tethered to a ship on the surface. It can dive to depths of 6,500 m (21,330 ft).

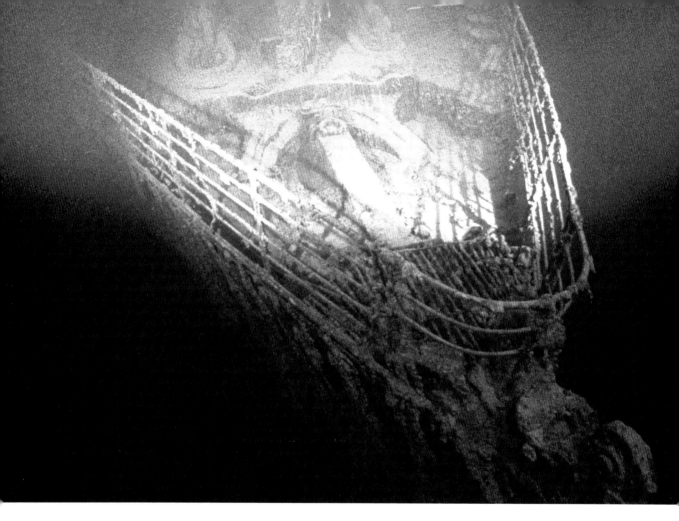

ALVIN'S ADVENTURES

Alvin has been involved in several famous ocean discoveries. In 1986, it carried explorers to the floor of the North Atlantic Ocean to visit the wreck of the passenger liner RMS *Titanic* for the first time. The ship, which sank after hitting an iceberg in 1912, had been located in 1985 using an ROV called *Argo*.

A decade earlier, in 1977, scientists on board *Alvin* made an amazing discovery as they explored the Galapagos Rift, a deep-ocean ridge in the Pacific Ocean. They found hydrothermal vents, where hot water spews out from under the ocean floor. The hot water is loaded with dissolved minerals that build up around the vents to form tall chimneys. Sometimes, the water from the vents is black with minerals, giving the vents the name "black smokers".

The scientists found previously unknown marine animals, such as tubeworms, thriving in the scalding, chemical-filled water around the vents. These animals changed scientific understanding of the way life works, as their food chain is not based on plants (see page 35). Today, *Alvin* and other submersibles are searching for new hydrothermal vents in places such as the Juan de Fuca Ridge off the northwestern United States, and the ridges of the central Pacific and the Arctic Oceans.

▲ *This photo of the railing at the bow (front end) of the sunken RMS* Titanic *was one of the first images the public saw of the famous shipwreck after it was explored using* Alvin *in 1986.*

▲ *Tubeworms living around a deep-ocean hydrothermal vent.*

EXPLORING A SEAMOUNT

In 2002, marine biologists used ROVs and AUVs (autonomous underwater vehicles), which are not tethered to a surface ship, to explore the Davidson Seamount in the Pacific Ocean off California, USA. This huge seamount rises from a depth of 3,650 m (11,980 ft) on the ocean floor. It is 2,400 m (7,870 feet) tall. The deep-ocean vessels tracked up and down the sides of the seamount, recording the different temperatures, types of animal, coral growth, and rock features at different depths.

WHO GOES EXPLORING?

Underwater exploration vehicles, and the ships that support them on the surface, are usually owned and run by research organizations such as the Woods Hole Oceanographic Institute (WHOI), based in Massachusetts, USA, or the Japan Agency for Marine-Earth Science and Technology (JAMSTEC). As well as sending their own scientists on deep-ocean missions, they lease out their vehicles and expertise to help film-makers, commercial companies, military forces, or archaeologists explore the ocean floor, too.

WHO'S WHO

Robert Ballard

Robert Ballard (born 1942) is a famous oceanographer and explorer who used the ROV *Argo* and the submersible *Alvin* to find and study the sunken wreck of the RMS *Titanic*. Working at WHOI in the 1960s, Ballard was one of the scientists who worked on the early stages of funding and building *Alvin*. In the 1970s, he worked with the navy, developing early ROVs. He dreamed of finding the RMS *Titanic* using these technologies. After a failed first attempt in 1977, he finally located it in 1985. He discovered the wreck at a depth of 3,800 m (12,500 ft) off Newfoundland, Canada, by sweeping the *Argo* ROV back and forth across the ocean floor. In 1986, he was one of the first to visit the wreck in person aboard *Alvin*.

IDEAS AND EXPERIMENTS

As well as going on new missions to explore the depths, oceanographers are busy developing new ways of exploring, and inventing new kinds of deep-ocean vehicles.

AUVS

AUVs are the latest generation of deep-ocean exploration vehicles. Like an ROV, an AUV, such as the *Odyssey III*, explores the deep oceans on its own, with no crew. But unlike an ROV, an AUV is not tethered to a ship. It is an underwater robot, programmed to be able to find its own way, and collect and record information by itself. It can then report its findings to the surface using radio signals. AUVs are often used like ROVs for one-off missions during explorations. But in the future, they will be able to go on longer and longer journeys, continuously mapping, sampling, and monitoring the oceans.

DEEP FLIGHT

A typical submersible uses heavy **ballast** and air tanks to change its **buoyancy**, allowing it to sink and rise slowly in the water. Now, a new kind of submersible, Deep Flight, designed to hold one person, is being developed. It works like a plane, with wings that allow it to "fly" up or down through the water. It moves faster than a conventional submersible, and is cheaper to use because it does not need a support ship on the surface. By saving money, Deep Flight and other similar submersibles could make deep-ocean exploration much easier.

DIVING HARD SUITS

In the quest to get closer to the underwater world they want to explore, scientists have returned to the diving suit, designing super-strong versions that can resist deep water pressure. They allow explorers or scientists to move freely into small spaces and get up close to wildlife. Engineers use them too, to do tricky jobs such as inspecting and mending deep-ocean structures and cables.

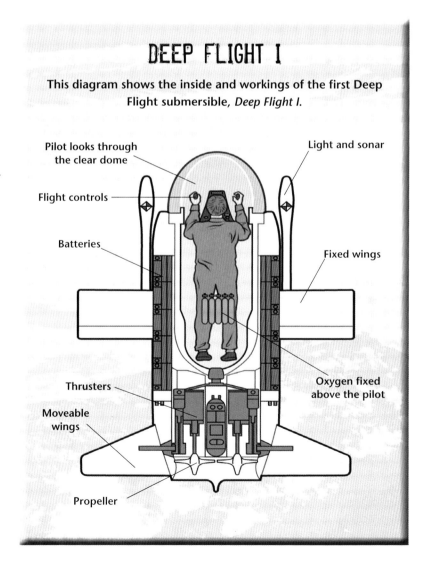

DEEP FLIGHT I

This diagram shows the inside and workings of the first Deep Flight submersible, *Deep Flight I*.

Pilot looks through the clear dome

Light and sonar

Flight controls

Batteries

Fixed wings

Thrusters

Moveable wings

Oxygen fixed above the pilot

Propeller

LIVING UNDERWATER

The great deep-ocean explorer Jacques Cousteau dreamed of being able to take exploration one step further, and live permanently underwater. In the 1960s, he built several underwater structures where divers could live for days at a time – known as the Conshelf Project. Conshelf was largely experimental, and is not still used today. However, there is an underwater science lab, called Aquarius, in water 20 m (65 ft) deep off the southern coast of Florida, USA. There, scientists can stay under water for 10-day-long diving missions to explore nearby coral reefs. The lab has a computer room, kitchen, bathroom facilities, and bunks for up to six people. More undersea labs like Aquarius could be developed, and perhaps stationed in much deeper water, to help scientists study deep-ocean wildlife, wrecks, and hydrothermal vents.

Cousteau's dream of whole underwater towns and cities has not yet come true – but it could still be a possibility, especially as rising sea levels (see page 13) threaten to engulf large areas of the Earth's land surface.

▲ *A view of the Aquarius lab in its position 20 m (65 ft) under the sea near coral reefs off the southern coast of Florida, USA.*

In their own words...

" It's really wonderful. You're living in this constantly beautiful blue environment. It's high pressure and close quarters inside, but you can go out in the reef and live at the same depth as the fish. You see the reef on its own terms, not the terms of the people diving from the top down. "

Greg Stone (born 1957), Vice President of the Global Marine Program at the New England Aquarium, USA, describes becoming an **aquanaut** on board Aquarius in 1999.

DEEP-OCEAN WILDLIFE

The oceans are the biggest habitats on Earth – they contain more than 97 percent of the Earth's living space, and more living things than any other kind of habitat. The oceans are home to almost every type of living thing, from tiny single-celled **algae** and **bacteria**, to sea snails, octopuses, crabs, reptiles, birds, and mammals, as well as thousands of species of fish.

ZONES OF LIFE

Life in the oceans is very different at different depths. In the sunlit zone, there are plenty of seaweeds and **phytoplankton** (microscopic sea plants). They provide food for animals, which in turn are eaten by other animals. The sunlit zone contains many different kinds of fish, whales and dolphins, jellyfish, and shellfish.

In the twilight zone, it is too dark for plants to grow. Some animals swim up closer to the surface at night to feed on plankton or plants. The rest are hunters. Twilight zone animals include various kinds of squid, prawns, whales, and fish, including several types of fierce sharks.

DEEP-OCEAN LIFE

In the total darkness of the dark, abyssal, and hadal zones, animals face a unique set of challenges. The deep ocean floor is covered with a thick layer of muddy silt called ooze, so some deep-ocean animals, such as sea cucumbers and sea spiders, have delicate legs for tiptoeing over it.

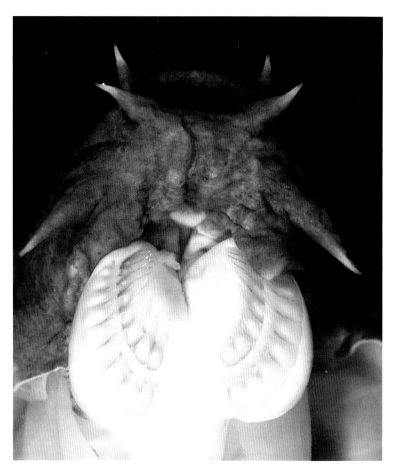

▲ Hagfish have many sharp teeth. The top of the photo shows the top of the hagfish's head, and the orange parts are the teeth. Some types of hagfish live on the ocean floor at depths of 1,000 m (3,300 ft) or deeper.

BIOLUMINESCENCE

Many deep-ocean animals are bioluminescent – they make their own light, and glow in various patterns and colours. In some deep-ocean fish, the light is actually given off by bioluminescent bacteria that live inside the fish's body. Some bioluminescent animals use the light to signal to each other. Others have a glowing lure that attracts smaller fish towards their mouths to be snapped up.

SEA MONSTERS

Sailors have told stories about huge, scary sea monsters for centuries. The seas and oceans are home to many of the world's biggest animals, such as the blue whale. Some of the "monsters" sailors have described may have been real sea animals, such as the giant squid or the giant octopus – perhaps made even bigger by exaggeration. Or, it could be that sailors really did see strange, monstrous sea animals that are still unknown to science.

Without plants, the main source of food is nutrient particles and dead animals that sink down from the sunlit zone. Many deep-ocean creatures, such as hagfish, are scavengers – they nibble and burrow into dead carcasses. The body of a large whale can last for up to 100 years after sinking to the deep ocean floor. Dead animals and plants decay very slowly in the deep oceans because it is so cold and there is little oxygen in the water.

HYDROTHERMAL VENT LIFE

Around hydrothermal vents (see pages 30–31), scientists have discovered living things that work completely differently from other life on Earth. Most living things ultimately depend on energy from the sun – sunlight makes plants grow, and plants form the basis of most food chains. But around hydrothermal vents, life is based on tiny bacteria that feed on minerals from inside the Earth. The minerals are dissolved in the hot water that churns out of the vents. In this way, the bacteria can survive without sunlight. Other, larger animals around the vents, such as tubeworms and clams, feed on nutrients provided by the bacteria, or on each other. These animals, unlike most, can also withstand the very high water temperatures around the vents, which have been measured at more than 110 degrees Celsius (°C) (230 degrees Fahrenheit [°F]).

▼ These two diagrams show a food chain based on plants, and another based on hydrothermal vent bacteria. Usually, food chains begin with sunlight. The hydrothermal vent food chain does not, and this is what makes it so unusual.

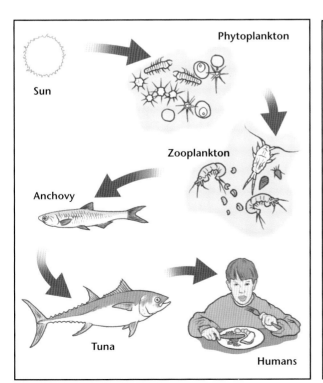

Sun
Phytoplankton
Zooplankton
Anchovy
Tuna
Humans

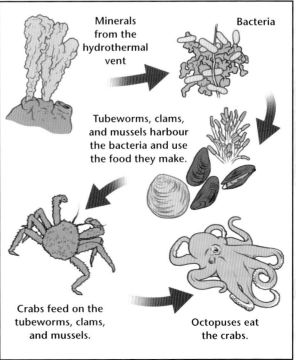

Minerals from the hydrothermal vent
Bacteria
Tubeworms, clams, and mussels harbour the bacteria and use the food they make.
Crabs feed on the tubeworms, clams, and mussels.
Octopuses eat the crabs.

▲ *The megamouth shark grows up to 5.2 m (17 ft) long, similar to a great white shark. However, it is not a fierce hunter. Instead, it uses its big mouth to collect plankton and shrimps from the water.*

DISCOVERING OCEAN ANIMALS

The deep oceans are so vast and hard to explore that all kinds of unknown animals can lurk there, waiting to be discovered. As oceanographers and marine biologists explore more and more of the oceans, they find more and more mysterious animals never before encountered. They range from tiny shrimps and jellyfish, to huge sharks and colossal squid.

THE MYSTERIOUS MEGAMOUTH

In 1976, a United States Navy ship off Oahu, Hawaii, pulled up its anchor and found a very large, strange deep-ocean shark entangled in it. The shark turned out to be a new species. It was named the "megamouth" shark (*Megachasma pelagios*) because of its huge mouth, lined with tiny teeth. To this day, only a few dozen megamouths have ever been seen, and only a handful of those have been observed alive. Only in the oceans could an animal as big as a megamouth go undetected for so long. Discoveries like this suggest that there are more big ocean animals still to be found.

DISCOVERY TIMELINE

Here are a few of the discoveries and sightings of previously unknown ocean wildlife in recent years:

1998: A new species of octopus, the mimic octopus, is found. It disguises itself by imitating other sea animals, such as sea snakes.

2001: A strange-looking, deep-ocean squid is found. It has thin, spidery tentacles and a mantle (body) shaped like a pair of wings.

2004: A new species of dragonfish is found. It is a small but fierce hunting fish with sharp teeth.

SEARCH FOR THE SUPERSQUID

Squid are fierce ocean predators related to octopuses. Little is known about many squid species, including the biggest squid of all. For many years the giant squid, a deep-sea dweller, was thought to be the largest. Including its tentacles, it may grow up to around 12 m (40 ft) long. Until very recently, though, knowledge of this squid came from dead specimens. In 2004, scientists finally found and filmed a living giant squid in the wild, near Japan.

In their own words...

"It was exciting to get a live tentacle. It was still functioning when we got it on the boat... The grip wasn't as strong as I expected; it felt sticky."

Dr. Tsunemi Kubodera, describing a squid tentacle that was accidentally cut off and left behind in his equipment.

However, another type of squid now looks as if it could be even bigger. Until 2003, the colossal squid was known only from a few body parts found inside whales' stomachs, but whole specimens found after 2003 showed it could grow to 14 m (46 ft). The heaviest one ever discovered was found in 2007 in the waters around Antarctica. It weighed an incredible 450 kilograms (kg) (990 pounds [lbs]).

MORE TO DISCOVER

Scientists are still searching for and studying unknown and rare sea animals. Some experts try to find or attract rare wildlife. One team used bait to attract a giant squid and filmed it with a camera lowered from a boat. Other scientists study unknown animals caught in fishing nets, or use submersibles (see page 28) to follow and watch underwater life in the wild.

▶ *This giant squid was washed up on a beach in Tasmania, Australia.*

SAVING THE OCEANS

Oceanographers studying the seas and oceans have seen them change enormously over the last 100 years. As they affect the weather, the **atmosphere**, and the food chain, the oceans are at the centre of the environmental problems facing the Earth.

OCEAN DESTRUCTION

Many different environmental problems are damaging the seas and oceans. To start with, they are being polluted by substances such as farm fertilizers, chemicals used in factories, and **sewage** from towns and cities. These run into rivers and flow into the oceans. Chemicals such as mercury can poison marine life, such as corals, or build up in animals' bodies and poison the animals that eat them. Litter is another type of pollution. Plastic rubbish from ships collects in the oceans where it is eaten by some animals, such as albatrosses. It can choke them or block their stomachs.

OVERFISHING

Overfishing means catching so many fish that some species can become **endangered**. In the past, overfishing mainly affected shallow-water species. But modern sonar and trawling technology allows fishing boats to find and catch shoals of deep-ocean fish, such as the orange roughy fish (*Hoplostethus atlanticus*), which lives at depths of around 1,400 m (4,600 ft). In the 1980s and 1990s, numbers of orange roughy plummeted.

▼ *This fishing crew are bringing in their catch of orange roughy.*

TEARING UP THE OCEAN FLOOR

As well as catching too many fish, trawling equipment, which works by dragging nets along the ocean floor, can damage it and tear up coral reefs. Reefs are not just found in warm, shallow seas – there are also cold-water coral reefs on the deep ocean floor. For example, the Darwin Mounds are humps of cold-water coral 1,000 m (3,300 ft) down on the ocean floor off the north of Scotland, UK. They provide food and shelter for many other deep-ocean species. Soon after they were discovered in 1998, scientists found that they were being badly damaged by trawling nets.

WARMER OCEANS

The oceans are also threatened by environmental changes, such as global warming (see page 13). Warmer water temperatures can kill some types of coral, for example, and make hurricanes more common and more severe. As the oceans heat up, some scientists think that the pattern of worldwide ocean currents could change. The Gulf Stream current (see page 10), for example, might "switch off" and stop flowing. This would change the climate and the habitats of thousands of ocean species.

▲ *This map, made from data collected by satellites, shows the surface temperature of the oceans. Red and orange show the warmest temperatures, and blue and purple the coldest.*

WHO'S WHO

Rachel Carson

Rachel Carson (1907–64) was an American marine biologist and environmentalist. She was one of the first scientists to raise awareness of the damage humans are doing to the planet. Her book *The Sea Around Us* tells the story of the sea, explaining how it formed and how it works. She also wrote another famous book, *Silent Spring*, about the dangers of chemicals such as pesticides. Today, she is seen as one of the founders of the environmental movement.

EXPLORING AND THE ENVIRONMENT

Earth's final frontiers are the few places where humans have barely set foot. They remain wildernesses because they are so hard to reach, and so we have mostly left them alone. By exploring them, we cannot help but disturb and change them in some way. Scientists and explorers must be careful to protect the habitats and wildlife they come across, and try to damage them as little as possible.

THE TROUBLE WITH TOURISM

Tourism means visiting a place for leisure or enjoyment. Many tourists are drawn to wild, "untouched" areas, especially near the seas and oceans, where they can escape from city life. The trouble is, tourists need hotels, restaurants, and transport, and these create pollution, which can affect ocean habitats and wildlife.

ECOTOURISM

Ecotourism is a form of tourism that aims to protect wild areas and wildlife, allowing tourists to visit them in controlled numbers. For example, ecotourists can go diving in the oceans to watch sharks feeding. This can help the environment, because it encourages local people to preserve marine species, rather than hunting them. However, even ecotourism still creates pollution and disturbs wildlife. Luckily, deep-ocean exploration is too expensive for ecotourism to happen much there – at least, so far.

▲ *Baby turtles are released into the sea in South Africa after being "notched" – having their shells marked – so that they can be monitored to keep track of their numbers. Studying the oceans helps scientists learn how to protect ocean wildlife.*

SCIENTIFIC EXPLORATION

Like tourists, scientists have to travel the world, causing pollution, in order to explore the oceans. Their submersibles and ROVs do disturb the ocean wilderness by landing on the ocean floor, taking rock samples, and introducing unfamiliar lights, sounds, and equipment into the deepest, darkest parts of the oceans.

DOING GOOD

Oceanographic study and discovery also help to work against environmental damage. For example, scientists track endangered marine species, such as sharks and turtles, and use their findings to campaign for laws that protect wildlife. Scientists also visit the deep seas and oceans to monitor pollution levels, currents, water temperature, polluting chemicals, litter, and sea levels. The information they bring back helps us to understand climate change and other environmental problems, so that we can begin to do something about them.

COMMERCIAL EXPLORATION

Oil and mineral companies dig under the ocean floor to look for useful mineral deposits. If they find deposits, they set up rigs and mining operations to extract them. In some cases this can damage the deep ocean floor and its **ecosystems**, by breaking up reefs, disturbing wildlife, and releasing dangerous substances into the water. Governments make laws to limit oil drilling and mining to just a few areas. They have also set up marine reserves – areas where no fishing or mining can take place – to protect some parts of the oceans.

SATELLITE TRACKING

Scientists use satellite tracking to monitor the movements of endangered species such as leatherback turtles. They fix a data recorder to the turtle's back, with an antenna that can send out radio signals when the turtle surfaces. The signals are picked up by satellites orbiting the Earth, and beamed back to the scientists' computers. The data recorder can also record information such as water temperature and pressure, so scientists can find out how deep the turtle has been diving. Leatherback turtles can dive to depths of more than 1,200 m (3,940 ft).

◀ A scientist tests a tracking device attached to a Weddell seal. One of the deepest-diving seals, it dives to depths of up to 600 m (2,000 ft) to hunt squid and octopuses.

FACTS AND STATISTICS

OCEAN EXPLORATION RECORDS

First deep-ocean dive: William Beebe and Otis Barton were the first to dive into the deep ocean, reaching a depth of 244 m (800 ft) in their bathysphere on 6 May 1931.

Deepest dive ever made by humans: Jacques Piccard and Don Walsh hold the record for diving deeper than any other humans. They visited the bottom of Challenger Deep, the deepest point in the oceans, on 23 January 1960, inside the bathyscaphe *Trieste*. At the time, the depth of their dive was recorded to be 10,916 m (35,813 ft), but more accurate measurements made in 1995 found that the maximum depth of Challenger Deep is 10,911 m (35,797 ft).

Deepest scuba dive: In 2005, diver Nuno Gomes made the deepest ever scuba dive, to a depth of just over 318 m (1,044 ft) in the Red Sea. He used weights to dive quickly, then returned to the surface slowly, so that he could gradually readjust to surface pressure.

OCEAN ANIMAL RECORDS

Biggest ocean animal: The blue whale (*Balaenoptera musculus*), which can grow up to 30 m (100 ft) long and weigh up to 136,400 kg (300,000 lbs), is the biggest ocean animal.

Longest-lived ocean animal: Scientists studying the deep-ocean tubeworm (*Lamellibrachia luymesi*) think that it can live for more than 250 years, making it among the longest-lived animals in the oceans.

Deepest-dwelling ocean animal: No one species is known to live deeper than all others, but we know that life exists at the deepest depths. When Jacques Piccard and Don Walsh arrived at the bottom of Challenger Deep in 1960, they saw a flatfish moving along the ocean floor, proving that fish live at these depths.

Deepest-diving air-breathing animal: The sperm whale (*Physeter macrocephalus*) is thought to be the animal that makes the deepest dives from the surface, holding its breath. Sonar equipment has spotted sperm whales hunting at depths of 2,500 m (8,200 ft).

AMAZING FACTS

More than 97 percent of all the water on Earth is in the seas and oceans.

Plants give out oxygen gas and soak up carbon dioxide gas, making the air healthy for humans and other animals to breathe. But it's not trees and forests that provide the most oxygen. The phytoplankton (plant plankton) in the seas and oceans provides more oxygen than all the rainforests and other forests combined.

The "Bloop" was a strange, very deep sound recorded in 1997 in the Pacific Ocean off South America. It sounded like an animal, but was so low and loud that scientists say any animal that made it would have to be huge – much bigger than the biggest known ocean animal, the blue whale.

There can be waterfalls in the oceans. The world's biggest known underwater waterfall is in the Denmark Strait off Greenland, where a flow of seawater falls 3.5 km (2.2 miles) towards the ocean floor. It is more than three times higher than the highest waterfall on land, Angel Falls in Venezuela.

If all the ice in Antarctica melted, the worldwide sea level would rise by about 60 m (197 ft).

The world's biggest ocean current, the Antarctic Circumpolar Current, moves 130 million cu m (4.5 billion cu ft) of water per second – more than all the world's rivers put together.

If we could extract all the gold from the world's seawater, everyone on Earth could have a large gold nugget weighing about 4 kg (9 lbs).

THE FIVE OCEANS

Pacific Ocean

Area	166 million square kilometres (sq km) (64 million sq miles), a third of Earth's surface and larger than Earth's entire land mass
Average depth	4,300 m (14,000 ft)
Deepest point	10,911 m (35,797 ft), at Challenger Deep in the Mariana Trench

Atlantic Ocean

Area	82 million sq km (32 million sq miles)
Average depth	3,330 m (10,930 ft)
Deepest point	8,605 m (28,230 ft), in the Puerto Rico Trench

Indian Ocean

Area	73.5 million sq km (28.4 million sq miles)
Average depth	3,890 m (12,760 ft)
Deepest point	8,047 m (26,400 ft), in the Diamantina Deep

Southern Ocean (sometimes called the Antarctic Ocean)

Area	20.3 million sq km (7.8 million sq miles)
Average depth	3,240 m (10,630 ft)
Deepest point	6,176 m (20,263 ft), in the South Sandwich Trench

Arctic Ocean

Area	14 million sq km (5.4 million sq miles)
Average depth	1,040 m (3,400 ft)
Deepest point	5,450 m (17,880 ft), in the Eurasian Basin

TIMELINE

c. 4.5 billion years ago Earth forms from dust, ice, and rocks in space.

c. 4 billion years ago Earth's seas and oceans form.

c. 40,000 BCE Early people use boats, probably dugout canoes made from logs, to travel the seas.

c. 4,000 BCE Ancient peoples dive without equipment to look for seafood, seashells, and sponges.

c. 360 BCE Ancient Greek writer, Aristotle, describes simple diving bells.

1620 Dutch inventor Cornelius Drebbel builds the first submarine out of wood and leather.

1837 German engineer Augustus Siebe invents the first diving suit.

1855 American oceanographer Matthew Fontaine Maury makes the first bathymetric map, showing the North Atlantic Ocean floor.

1872–76 The ship HMS *Challenger* travels the globe studying the oceans and charting the ocean floor.

1900–20 Sonar technology is developed, allowing very accurate ocean depth measurements.

1931 William Beebe and Otis Barton make the first deep-ocean dive to 244 m (800 ft) in their deep-ocean diving vessel, the bathysphere.

1932–54 HMS *Challenger II* uses sonar bathymetry to map the world's ocean floors.

1934 Beebe and Barton make their deepest bathysphere dive, to 923 m (3,028 ft).

1943 French explorers Jacques Cousteau and Emile Gagnan invent the aqualung.

1946–48 Swiss explorer Auguste Piccard builds his first bathyscaphe, a kind of deep-ocean diving machine.

1960 Piccard's bathyscaphe *Trieste* makes the deepest dive ever, to 10,911 m (35,797 ft).

1964 The first deep-ocean submersible, *Alvin*, is launched.

1969 *Alvin* sinks and is lost on the ocean floor for three months before being recovered.

1973 The first ROV is developed.

1977 Hydrothermal vents are discovered on the ocean floor near the Galapagos Islands.

1992 The Aquarius underwater lab is stationed near coral reefs in the sea off Florida, USA.

2004 The giant squid is filmed in the wild for the first time.

2005 ROV *Scorpio 45* is used to free a Russian submarine trapped underwater, saving seven lives.

FURTHER RESOURCES

BOOKS

Secrets of the Deep Revealed, Frances Dipper, Dorling Kindersley, 2003

National Geographic Atlas of the Ocean, Sylvia Earle, National Geographic Society, 2001

Ocean: The World's Last Wilderness Revealed, Rob Houston, Dorling Kindersley, 2006

Diving to a Deep-Sea Volcano, Kenneth Mallory, Houghton Mifflin Co., 2006

Philip's Guide to the Oceans, Dr. John Pernetta, Philip's, 2004

Oceans: Surviving in the Deep Sea, Michael Sandler, Bearport Publishing, 2005

Amazing Journeys: To the Depths of the Ocean, Rod Theodorou, Heinemann Library, 2006

WEBSITES

http://oceanexplorer.noaa.gov/welcome.html
Lots of information about ocean exploration

www.pbs.org/wgbh/nova/abyss/
Information about travelling into the abyssal zone

http://school.discovery.com/schooladventures/planetocean/ocean.html
Amazing facts about the oceans of our planet

www.pmel.noaa.gov/vents/acoustics/sounds/bloop.html
Listen to the recording of the "Bloop".

GLOSSARY

abyssal plain mainly flat ocean floor, between depths of 4,000 m (13,000 ft) and 6,000 m (20,000 ft), that forms the bottom of most oceans

abyssal zone ocean depth between about 4,000 m (13,000 ft) and the abyssal plain

adaptation change to fit new conditions

algae simple, often microscopic plant-like organisms that use sunlight to live and grow

aqualung diving equipment that uses a valve to regulate a supply of pressurized air or oxygen for a diver to breathe

aquanaut person who lives underwater or spends periods of more than 24 hours there

asteroid lump of rock from space

atmosphere layer of gases surrounding Earth, held there by gravity

atmosphere (atm) unit of pressure – one atmosphere is equal to the air pressure at sea level

bacteria very small, single-celled living things found in most habitats

ballast heavy weights used to weigh down a floating vessel, such as a ship or submersible

basin low-lying, bowl-shaped area of the ocean floor

bathymetry measuring and charting the ocean floor

bathyscaphe deep-ocean diving vessel with a pressurized passenger chamber attached to a floatation tank

bathysphere deep-ocean diving vessel consisting of a heavy iron sphere lowered on a cable from a support ship

buoyancy force that makes an object float in a fluid that is denser than itself

claustrophobic closed-in space that can make people frightened

condense change from a gas into a liquid

continental crust layer of rock that forms Earth's continents

continental rise area of gently sloping ocean floor, connecting the abyssal plain to the continental slope

continental shelf area of shallow, gently sloping ocean floor surrounding most continents

continental slope sloping ocean floor that leads from the continental shelf down to the abyssal plain

continents Earth's main land masses

current flow or stream of water within a larger body of water

cyclone hurricane, especially in the Pacific or Indian Ocean

dark zone ocean depth zone between about 1,000 m (3,300 ft) and 4,000 m (13,000 ft)

diving bell diving vessel shaped like a bell or an upturned cup, with an open base, that traps a pocket of air when lowered into the water

ecosystem community made up of a habitat and the plants and animals that live together in it

endangered in danger of dying out

evaporate change from a liquid into a gas

glacier slow-moving mass of ice that flows downhill

gulf large area of sea mainly enclosed by land

habitat environment where living things are found

hadal zone ocean depth below 6,000 m (20,000 ft), usually found in deep-ocean trenches

hurricane powerful, swirling storm that forms over warm ocean surfaces

hydrothermal vent hole in the ocean floor where underground water heated by magma inside the Earth flows out into the ocean

ice age period of colder temperatures in Earth's history during which large parts of the Earth were covered by ice and snow

ice cap mass of ice permanently covering an area of land, such as Antarctica

oceanic crust layer of rock that forms the Earth's ocean floors

ooze layer of slimy sediment on the ocean floor, mostly made up of the remains of tiny plankton animals

phytoplankton plant-like plankton that uses sunlight to make its own food

plankton mass of mainly very small living things that drifts around in ocean water

precipitation rain, or water in any other form, that falls from the sky to the ground

prospector someone who searches for valuable resources, such as useful minerals, in order to mine or harvest them

ridge long, raised section of the ocean floor, formed by volcanic activity where two tectonic plates are moving apart

satellite spacecraft in orbit around Earth, often used to collect data or send messages

scuba short for Self-Contained Underwater Breathing Apparatus, another name for aqualung diving equipment

seamount mountain on the ocean floor

sediment mud, sand, and silt that sinks down and settles into layers, especially on the ocean floor

sedimentology study of sediment

seep crack in the ocean floor where hot water from inside Earth trickles out slowly

sewage waste from toilets and drains

silt muddy material made up of fine particles

sounding measuring the depth of water

strait narrow channel connecting two seas or oceans

submersible small, deep-sea diving vessel that can carry passengers and explore on its own, without being connected to the surface

sunlit zone shallowest ocean depth area, between the surface and a depth of 200 m (650 ft)

tectonic plates huge, jigsaw-like sections of rock that make up the Earth's crust

transponder device placed on the ocean floor to act as a marker that submersibles use to calculate their position

trench long, low-lying section of the ocean floor, usually formed by one tectonic plate pushing down beneath another

tsunami series of powerful waves caused by a sudden movement of a large amount of seawater

twilight zone ocean depth area between about 200 m (650 ft) and 1,000 m (3,300 ft)

typhoon hurricane, especially in the Pacific or Indian Ocean

INDEX